Now Is the Time

Now Is the Time

Patrick Lindsay

hardie grant books
MELBOURNE · LONDON

Published in 2009
by Hardie Grant Books
85 High Street
Prahran, Victoria 3181, Australia
www.hardiegrant.com.au

A catalogue record for this book is available from the National
Library of Australia.

ISBN: 978 1 74066 654 1

Jacket design and illustration by Marie Doucette
Typeset by Nathan Hayward
Printed and bound in China by C&C Offset Printing

For Lisa, Nathan, Kate and Sarah ... as always

Now is the time to...

tame your inbox

Stop allowing email to dominate your life.
It interrupts your concentration.
It puts you in a state of constant anticipation.
Break the cycle. Disconnect.
Treat it like snail mail.
Check it once each morning and late afternoon.
Give yourself time to think.

'Information is pretty thin stuff, unless mixed with experience.'
Clarence Day (1874–1935)

Now is the time to...

lighten your load

Make sure you're only carrying today's burdens.
Too often we carry far more than necessary.
Reduce your load by dropping tomorrow's worries,
and yesterday's baggage.
Present pressures and problems are usually enough.
Leave tomorrow's until later.

'Every morning cries to us: Do what you ought and trust what may be.'
Johann Wolfgang von Goethe (1749–1832)

choose freedom

Too often we make our own cages:
of the mind, or the heart.
Or we allow technology to make them for us.
But we have the keys to unlock them.
We only need the will to use them.
Unlock your heart, love freely.
Unlock your mind, live freely.

'The secret of happiness is freedom. The secret of freedom is courage.'
Thucydides (460–404 BC)

Now is the time to...

enjoy the day

Make the most of every day.
Use up the hours like a child.
There are no guarantees how many we get.
Older people will tell you
they rarely regret the things they did,
only the things they didn't do.
Don't spend your life intending to do something.
Start now!

'And in the end, it's not the years in your life that count, it's the life in your years.'

Abraham Lincoln (1809–1865)

Now is the time to...

cherish your family

They may exasperate and infuriate us.
But they are one of our most precious possessions.
Don't take them for granted.
We never know how long we will have them,
or they us.
They are our mirror and our anchor.
Treasure your time with them.

'The family is the country of the heart.'

Giuseppe Mazzini (1805–1872)

Now is the time to...

take the first step

The longest journey, or project, starts with a first step.
When it's too hard to picture the whole journey,
break it down into smaller ones.
Keep reducing until the first step seems attainable.
Then take it.
The others will follow.

'To begin, begin.'

Peter Nivio Zarlenga (1941–)

Now is the time to...

be you

Our greatest journey is our internal voyage.
Take time to discover yourself.
Find your essence, the unique you.
Advertisers want to classify you.
They want you to conform, to be part of a group.
You are an individual.
Live your own life.

'Your time is limited, so don't waste it living someone else's life.'
Steve Jobs (1955–)

rekindle your imagination

Reality often swamps us
and paralyses our imagination.
Sometimes we need to hit the pause button.
We need to find time to let our minds play,
relax, regenerate.
Give your mind a treat.
Find a sanctuary. Close your eyes.
Shut out the real world.
Let your mind create its own.
Enjoy the trip.

'I shut my eyes in order to see.'

Paul Gauguin (1848–1903)

take responsibility

It's easy to hide in a crowd
but it's so unsatisfying.
It leads to a life of desperation and griping
because others are making your life choices,
and you are following.
Take control of your life.
Make your own decisions.
Take responsibility for them.
Proudly chart your own course.

'No snowflake in an avalanche ever feels responsible.'
Voltaire (1694–1778)

persevere

Those who succeed usually have
one big thing in common:
they never give up.
No matter how long it takes,
no matter how many obstacles in their way,
they fight on until they prevail.
Above so many things,
perseverance is vital to success.

'Continuous effort – not strength or intelligence – is the key to
unlocking our potential.'

Sir Winston Churchill (1874–1965)

Now is the time to...

read a classic

They stand the test of time for good reason.
They transport you to another world.
There, you can forget your troubles.
You can vicariously live other lives –
run risks, feel thrills, meet heroes, see horrors –
all from the safety of your imagination.

'A great book should leave you with many experiences, and slightly exhausted. You should lead several lives while reading it.'
William Styron (1925–2006)

embrace your problems

Take a different view of the challenges in your life:
as opportunities to become a stronger person.
See them as stepping stones on your journey.
Use them to strengthen your resolve,
to gain wisdom and compassion.
Enjoy the satisfaction of overcoming them
and pushing your personal boundaries.

'On a calm sea every man is a pilot.'

English proverb

Now is the time to...

go on a data diet

We live under constant information bombardment.
Give yourself a chance to
discern the good from the useless.
Limit the stream of data to which you're exposed.
Take time out from your computer.
Turn off the TV.
Make your holiday a real one:
cut the information chain.
Only consume gourmet data.

'Information – in the sense of raw data – is not knowledge; that knowledge is not wisdom; and that wisdom is not foresight. But information is the first essential step to all of these.'
Arthur C. Clarke (1917–2008)

Now is the time to...

give yourself some space

Look at the walls surrounding you.
Real or imaginary, they limit your potential.
Push through them by using your downtime wisely.
Expand your horizons.
Visit new places.
Develop new skills.
Enrich yourself.

'Make the most of yourself, for that is all there is of you.'
Ralph Waldo Emerson (1803–1882)

Now is the time to...

get a good night's sleep

Break the cycles:
of working late, mindless TV, nights out.
Reconnect with your body.
Show it some respect.
Recharge your batteries.
Savour the results.

'It is a common experience that a problem difficult at night is resolved
in the morning after the committee of sleep has worked on it.'
John Steinbeck (1902–1968)

Now is the time to...

watch what you eat

It's not complicated.
It's just old-fashioned common sense.
We all overeat.
We know we're doing it.
We regret it immediately.
Think about it:
how often have we ever been at risk of starving?
We feel most alert and alive when we eat frugally.
Give it a try.
If you have doubts,
make a list of everything you eat for a week.
It will shock and motivate you!

'To lengthen thy life, lessen thy meals.'

Benjamin Franklin (1706–1790)

Now is the time to...

care for our planet

We're all shareholders in our earth,
even if our holding may seem tiny.
But one by one, then together,
we can make a difference.
We hold its future in our hands.
Even the smallest individual kindnesses count,
when multiplied by mankind.
Make your commitment.
Play your role.

'We do not inherit the land from our ancestors, we borrow it from our children.'

Native American proverb

Now is the time to...

chart a new course

We are all creatures of routine.
Start to think outside of your normal boundaries.
Start small:
a new route to work,
lunch at a new café,
a chat with strangers.
Then look further afield:
join a club, help a charity, plan a trip, start a new hobby.
Grow.

'Do not go where the path may lead, go instead where there is no
path and leave a trail.'

Ralph Waldo Emerson (1803–1883)

Now is the time to...

ask questions

Often we feel powerless.
Like tiny cogs in a giant machine.
But we can acquire power:
by challenging things we doubt or know to be untrue.
Each intelligent question helps.
It strengthens the individual.
It humanises the process.

'A foolish faith in authority is the worst enemy of truth.'
Albert Einstein (1879–1955)

Now is the time to...

take the wide view

Look as a photographer does.
Use all your lenses and change your position:
from close-up to wide-angle,
from aerial to x-ray.
Take in the small things
but zoom out to see the full picture.
Look beyond the obvious.
Relish the complexities and the relationships.

'If the doors of perception were cleansed everything would appear to man as it is, infinite.'

William Blake (1757–1827)

Now is the time to...

discover your forte

We all have a special gift or forte.
Some find it early.
For others, the discovery is more difficult.
Your forte is where you naturally shine.
It's where you express yourself best:
where you can allow your passions full rein.
Allow your forte to assert itself.

'The fox knows many things but the hedgehog only knows one big thing.'

Archilochus (seventh century BC)

Now is the time to...

find your moral compass

We know in our heart of hearts what is right.
We can choose to ignore the feeling or to act on it.
But when we ignore it, we feel incomplete.
We know we have sold ourselves short.
It takes courage – sometimes great courage –
but when we follow our conscience
we find real freedom.

'The hottest places in hell are reserved for those who, in times of great moral crisis, maintain their neutrality.'

Dante Alighieri (1265–1321)

Now is the time to...

tread lightly

Everywhere we look mankind is riding
roughshod over the earth.
Wherever we can, we must preserve nature.
Each individual gesture matters.
Millions of small gestures become a massive force.
However you can, wherever you can, make the effort:
for yourself,
for your children,
for their children.

'In wilderness is the preservation of the world.'
Henry David Thoreau (1817–1862)

Now is the time to...

focus your energy

We are constantly faced with competing demands,
and easily distracted by the noise and the interruptions.
To be effective in our lives and work, we must focus.
We must decide on our priorities.
We must channel our energy,
and attend to the task before us.

'Think of many things, do only one.'

English proverb

Now is the time to...

think of others

We're encouraged to think of ourselves,
our needs, our desires.
The media, advertisers, gurus all add to this impetus.
But real satisfaction comes elsewhere.
Genuine growth and priceless enjoyment
come from helping others.
Look where you can help.
Do it with selfless passion.
Enjoy the feeling.

'Only a life lived for others is worth living.'

Albert Einstein (1879–1955)

Now is the time to...

act

When you know the right path, take it.
Too often we wait for the perfect moment.
And we miss the opportunity.
Use your senses, back your judgement.
Decisiveness offers many rewards.

'Defer no time, delays have dangerous ends.'
William Shakespeare (1564–1616)

Now is the time to...

learn

Each day we meet someone new.
We're exposed to new thoughts, new ways.
Use every opportunity to add to your knowledge.
Go with an open mind.
Relish the chance to learn.
Enjoy the challenge.
Seek perspective.

'I do not think much of a man who is not wiser today than he was yesterday.'

Abraham Lincoln (1809–1865)

Now is the time to...

commit yourself

Those who succeed set themselves
apart by their commitment.
Most of us make an effort:
we prepare; we try; but then we hope.
If you really want to achieve something,
you must be prepared to stretch yourself.
You must distil your energy and focus all your efforts.
You must give of yourself.

'If you're not actively involved in getting what you want, you don't
really want it.'

Peter McWilliams (1949–)

Now is the time to...

take control of your life

We all have restrictions in our lives.
But, equally, we all have vast areas of untested capacity:
to make decisions, to plan our future,
to follow our paths.
It's easy to blame others for our inaction.
It's easy to blame our constraints.
Take the initiative.
Take control.
Decide your own journey.

'Work out your own salvation. Do not depend on others.'
Buddha (563–483 BC)

Now is the time to...

have a go!

Australians have a saying: 'Have a go!'
It means stop hesitating and make a determined effort.
Too often we are hamstrung by fear of failure.
Or we hold back, waiting for the perfect moment.
Sometimes, we should just give it our best shot.
You'll be proud of your decisiveness.
Others will admire your courage.

'Fortune favours the bold.' (Audaces fortuna iuvat.)

Latin proverb

Now is the time to...

seek advice

It must be from a respected source,
and balanced against your own
knowledge and instincts.
But seeking advice brings many rewards:
it honours the giver;
it enhances the receiver;
it creates perspective.

'Wise men don't need advice. Fools won't take it.'
Benjamin Franklin (1706–1790)

Now is the time to...

learn from your anger

It often pays to look back in serenity at your anger.
Pent-up emotions can reveal unseen messages.
And anger may be driven by deep insight.
Consider your motivation.
Examine the underlying triggers.
Learn the lessons.

'The tigers of wrath are wiser than the horses of instruction.'
William Blake (1757–1827)

Now is the time to...

unleash your imagination

The power of our minds is virtually unlimited
and largely untapped.
With imagination we can create new worlds
and improve old ones.
We can live our wildest dreams
and dream our wildest lives.

'The fairest souls are those that have the most variety and
adaptability.'

Michel de Montaigne (1533–1592)

Now is the time to...

be a mentor

This can bring unexpected benefits:
you pass on your hard-won skills and wisdom,
you receive great insight and friendship,
you become a conduit for wisdom.
You light the way for another.
In return, you see life through different eyes
and, usually, you'll learn more than you'll teach.

'By learning you will teach, by teaching you will learn.'

Latin proverb

Now is the time to...

volunteer your time

Volunteers form the backbone of our communities.
They set the tone for our culture.
Volunteering brings help and guidance to recipients
and great satisfaction to the givers.
It fills a spiritual void.
It builds friendships, creates confidence
and promotes natural leadership.

'He who doesn't think too much of himself is much more esteemed
than he imagines.'

Johann Wolfgang von Goethe (1749–1832)

Now is the time to...

spread love

Giving love binds us.
It validates our lives.
It gives us meaning.
It brings compassion.
It gives us new eyes.

'To love someone deeply gives you strength, being loved by someone
deeply gives you courage.'

Lao Tse (circa 600 BC)

Now is the time to...

be flexible

Be patient.
Keep your mind open.
Don't rush to conclusions.
Be wary of unshakeable certainty.
Allow for unthought-of possibilities.
You will broaden your vision
and strengthen your judgement.

'Time cools, time clarifies; no mood can be maintained quite unaltered through the course of hours.'

Thomas Mann (1875–1955)

Now is the time to...

find your tribe

We all have a natural habitat:
in the country, by the sea, in the city.
It's in our blood, our natural homeland.
It's where we're most content,
where we flourish.
It's where we find peace.

'It is in the shelter of each other that people live.'

Irish proverb

Now is the time to...

break the cycle

Challenge the routines in your life.
Seek a sanctuary.
Pause and reflect.
Find the monotonies and change them.
Take new paths.
Try new ways.
Chill.
Return recharged.

'To enjoy life we must touch much of it lightly.'

Voltaire (1694–1778)

Now is the time to...

prepare

How often do we start something
without any homework?
Yet preparation is usually all that's within our control.
We waste countless hours by ignoring it.
Whatever the project, think ahead:
consider its needs, its problems, its shortcuts.
Give yourself every advantage.
Build your confidence, create options.
Time spent doing this will be handsomely rewarded.

'If I had eight hours to chop down a tree, I'd spend six hours
sharpening my axe.'

Abraham Lincoln (1809–1865)

seek authenticity

Be genuine.
Be the person you are inside.
Look for authenticity in others.
Praise it.
Encourage it.
Emulate it.
It will attract a matching response.
It will set you apart.

'The mass of men live lives of quiet desperation.'
Henry David Thoreau (1817–1862)

listen to your heart

Connect your head to your heart.
Learn to trust your heart's instincts.
Be open to its signals.
Heed them.
Act on them.

'All the knowledge I possess everyone else can acquire, but my heart is
exclusively my own.'

Johann Wolfgang von Goethe (1749–1832)

Now is the time to...

start again

Look at nature:
nothing stays the same.
Use change to your advantage.
Keep the things that matter.
Change the things that don't.
Like a sporting champion,
change a losing game.
Then start afresh.

'Go out as far as you can go and start from there'
Albert Einstein (1879–1955)

Now is the time to...

rebound

From time to time we all suffer reverses.
Sometimes they seem overwhelming or endless.
But only if you look at them in isolation.
Things come in cycles:
what goes around comes around.
Bide your time. Bounce back.

'Our greatest glory is not in never failing but in rising every time we
fall.'

Confucius (551–479 BC)

Now is the time to...

find beauty

Beauty surrounds us.
But it's not always evident.
Seek it out.
Find it in love, friendship, nature, art.
See it in another's mind or spirit.
Look for the inner glow.

'A heart in love with beauty never grows old.'

Turkish proverb

Now is the time to...

show your manners

Good manners are a civilising force.
They command attention.
They have an innate beauty.
They bestow respect.
They reveal character.
They invite reciprocity.

'If a man be gracious and courteous to strangers, it shows he is a citizen of the world.'

Francis Bacon (1561–1626)

use your wisdom

Wisdom is the ability to use experience
to gain perspective.
We all have unique experiences.
The trick is to use the knowledge we gain from it:
to draw on it for guidance in different circumstances;
to see the relationships between things.
Allow yourself to use your experience.

'Intuition is nothing but the outcome of earlier intellectual experience.'
Albert Einstein (1879–1955)

Now is the time to...

fight for justice

Injustice surrounds us, at home and abroad.
We can try to ignore it.
Or we can use our influence to fight it.
Stand up when you know something is wrong.
Support those fighting for right.
We don't have to be heroes,
or even be in the front line.
But if we expect justice for ourselves,
we must support it for others.

'In the struggle for social justice, impatience is essential.'
John Gardner (1912–2002)

Now is the time to...

confront your fears

Our fears are our chains,
but only while we empower them.
Don't underestimate your courage.
If necessary, face things in stages,
and gain strength from your progress.
Often our fear is outdated
or based on misunderstanding.
Challenge your fears.
Break their spell and you're free.

'Courage is the mastery of fear, not the absence of fear.'
Mark Twain (1835–1910)

Now is the time to...

watch the sun rise

To feel the real beauty and power of the sun,
rise before the first rays hit.
Find a vantage point with a fine vista and wait.
Sense the stillness.
Watch as the sun etches out your world.
Enjoy the warmth.
Marvel at the miracle of renewal.
Feel your problems subside.

'Turn your face to the sun and the shadows will fall behind you.'
Maori proverb

Now is the time to...

make your vote count

Politics may be show business for ugly people,
but we must still take part in the selection process.
Think of those who have no vote,
no power to control their destiny.
Honour them by using your vote wisely.
Whether national, state or local elections,
study the candidates and their policies.
Make a reasoned selection.

'Votes should be weighed, not counted.'
Friedrich von Schiller (1759–1805)

Now is the time to...

support an artist

They bring beauty into our world.
They look at things differently.
They allow us to see ourselves differently.
They inspire us to be more creative.
Yet very few of them make good livings.
They enhance our lives and deserve encouragement.
Look for those who move you.
Support them where you can.

'The artist must have something to say.'
Wassily Kandinsky (1866–1944)

Now is the time to...

treasure your memories

We each have a unique album of personal memories:
mental snapshots of the key moments in our lives.
Every so often, look through your album.
Relive them.
Learn from them.
Hand them down to your kids.
Then go and add to them.

'Every man's memory is his private literature.'
Aldous Huxley (1894–1963)

Now is the time to...

have faith

In our cynical world, faith is ever more important.
Nurture your faith:
in yourself, in your beliefs, in love, in kindness.
Recognise its mystical powers.
Embrace it.
Use its strength.

'Faith is the bird that feels the light and sings when the dawn is still
dark.'

Rabindranath Tagore (1861–1941)

Now is the time to...

nurture your creativity

We are all creative.
We are all artists of some kind.
Some are better than others,
a few are geniuses.
But we all have a creative spirit.
Allow it to rise up.
Nurture it, challenge it.
Give it freedom.
Celebrate it.

'Love the art in yourself, not yourself in the art.'
Konstantin Stanislavsky (1863–1938)

Now is the time to...

celebrate elegance

Understated, natural elegance is entrancing.
It's an underrated virtue,
a thing of lasting beauty.
In dress, in speech, in art, in sport, in living,
elegance enriches us all.
It's unforgettable.
It transcends the ages.
Pursue it.

'A truly elegant taste is generally accompanied with excellency of
heart.'

Henry Fielding (1707–1754)

Now is the time to...

use your experience

In a world obsessed with youth,
experience is often undervalued.
But your unique experiences are priceless.
They give you many advantages.
Cherish them.
Use them wisely:
at work, with your family,
in relationships, in planning ahead.

'The older the fiddle, the sweeter the tune.'

English proverb

look at the positives

It's easy to let our problems dominate us,
to allow them to overshadow our good fortune.
Look broadly at your life.
Bring the positives to the fore:
the love of your family, your partner, your friends,
your achievements, at work, at home.
Change your point of view:
feel how it empowers you.

'I felt sorry for myself because I had no shoes, until I met a man who had no feet.'

Jewish proverb

Now is the time to...

keep trying

When things are not going our way,
it's tempting to sit back and wait.
But then, more than ever, we must renew our efforts.
Believe in yourself.
Back your judgement.
Push through your protective boundaries.
Keep going.

'The dog that trots about finds a bone.'

Gypsy proverb

Now is the time to...

savour the seasons

Welcome the variety in nature,
its ever-changing cycles.
They make sense of growth and death and decay.
They bring hope and renewal.
They give us a glimpse of eternity.
Their relentless passage brings optimism
and harmony.

'For him in vain the envious seasons roll,
Who bears eternal summer in his soul.'
Oliver Wendell Holmes (1809–1894)

Now is the time to...

think deeply

How often we act without thinking,
and suffer the consequences.
Take time to consider.
Avoid distraction, concentrate.
Slowly wash problems through your mind.
Consider the consequences.
Develop options.
Look ahead.
Then decide.

'I think and think for months and years. Ninety-nine times, the
conclusion is false. The hundredth time I am right.'
Albert Einstein (1879–1955)

Now is the time to...

take the initiative

Never underestimate your potential.
Give yourself the best chance to fulfil it:
chart your own course.
Stop allowing others to dictate your actions
– or reactions.
Stop being a passive critic.
When you know the right course of action,
take it.

'It is better to be making the news than taking it; to be an actor rather than a critic.'

Winston Churchill (1874–1965)

Now is the time to...

see the funny side

Look for the humour, however dire the situation.
It will break the tension.
It will clear your mind.
It will bring perspective and enhance understanding.
It can keep violence at bay,
and soothe the wounded.
Life is too short not to laugh.

'The most wasted day of all is that on which we have not laughed.'
Sebastien de Chamfort (1741–1794)

appreciate greatness

Some people deserve our admiration.
Too often we deny it to them
because of jealousy or cynicism.
Give respect and admiration where it is due.
Men like Nelson Mandela and women
like Mother Teresa epitomise greatness.
Acknowledging their greatness does them,
and us, credit.

'No sadder proof can be given by a man of his own littleness than disbelief in great men.'

Thomas Carlyle (1795–1881)

Now is the time to...

observe nature

Nature is a wonderful teacher.
Whether you live in the city or the wilderness,
lessons abound.
See how nature adapts to the changing world around it.
Admire its persistence
and marvel at its resilience.
Appreciate.

'Adapt or perish, now as ever, is nature's inexorable imperative.'
H.G. Wells (1866–1946)

Now is the time to...

make a decision

We procrastinate too often:
reconsidering, torturing ourselves with indecision.
Governments do it by establishing boards of inquiries.
Golfers call it paralysis by analysis.
It's better to think things through, then decide.
Correcting an error is less painful
than being trapped on the fence.

'One foot can't stand on two boats.'

Chinese proverb

Now is the time to...

lose your fear of failure

Failing simply improves your chances
of succeeding next time.
You can't make progress without failing.
But fear of failure is our greatest brake:
to growth, to knowledge, to progress.
Allow yourself the possibility of failure.
Feel the liberation it brings.

'To conquer oneself is a greater task than conquering others.'
Buddha (563–483 BC)

Now is the time to...

stick together

A winning team is greater than the sum of its parts.
Form great teams:
with your partner, with your family, at work, at play.
Revel in the power of the team.
Enjoy the selfless satisfaction it brings.
Explore the boundaries it pushes through.

'All for one, one for all, that's our device.'
Alexandre Dumas (1802–1870), The Three Musketeers

Now is the time to...

explore online

Like an ancient mariner,
use your computer to find new worlds.
Explore places you've only read about.
Learn about people and their countries.
Shrink the world.
Understand other lives.
Enrich your own.

'Man's mind, once stretched by a new idea, never regains its original dimensions.'

Oliver Wendell Holmes (1841–1935)

Now is the time to...

look beyond the obvious

Look behind the news.
Put things in perspective.
Search for relationships, root out bias.
Peer through opinion to find the factual foundations.
Test assumptions.
Pose questions.
Demand answers.

'The pure and simple truth is rarely pure and never simple.'
Oscar Wilde (1854–1900)

Now is the time to...

find your inner leader

It comes naturally to some.
To most, it's cloaked in self-doubt and fear.
But we all have an inner leader.
Whether it be on the big stage or in our private world,
as a parent, a partner, a friend, a mentor.
The power is within us.

'A man who has confidence in himself wins the confidence of others.'
Jewish proverb

Now is the time to...

chase your dream

We make our own limitations:
through self-doubt, fear and conformity.
But we can also expand our horizons.
We can push through the barriers, real and imagined.
If you have a dream,
give it a chance.
Empower yourself.

'The truth lies in a man's dreams.'

Miguel de Cervantes (1547–1616)

Now is the time to...

use your talents

We all have talents,
in different fields and in differing degrees.
The trick is to make the most of them.
Some come naturally.
Most come through hard work.
But having talent is just the start,
using talent to fulfil potential is most difficult –
and most admirable.

'Since talent is so often scar tissue over a wound, perhaps I had more
than most men.'

Elia Kazan (1909–2003)

Now is the time to...

ignore your limitations

Limitations are just guideposts.
They may signal different routes
or different ways to reach a destination.
But they won't prevent us from getting there,
unless we empower them to do so.
Ignore them,
focus on the journey.

'I seldom think about my limitations, and they never make me sad.'
Helen Keller (1880–1968)

Now is the time to...

live to fight another day

The temptation is always to fight to the bitter end.
But sometimes it's wiser to take the longer view.
When a situation is irreparable,
or the circumstances have changed dramatically,
it may be better to cut your losses.
Acknowledge the mistake.
Learn the lesson.
Salvage the position.
Live to fight another day.

'Better to lose the anchor than to lose the whole ship.'
Danish proverb

Now is the time to...

think things through

Resist the pressure to react without consideration.
Pause to see things in perspective.
Think through your options.
Give weight to the consequences of your action.
But when you decide,
act with dispatch.

'Think like a man of action and act like a man of thought.'
Henri Bergson (1859–1941)

Now is the time to...

add spice to your relationship

Make a conscious effort to honour your loved one.
Start with the little things:
a hug, a kiss, flowers, a card, a note, a small gift.
Then remember the bigger things:
their feelings, their hopes, their needs, their goals.
Set aside time for each other.
Keep alert to each other's feelings and moods.
Keep the relationship young and fresh.

'How do I love thee? Let me count the ways.'
Elizabeth Barrett Browning (1806–1861)

Now is the time to...

look for hidden opportunities

The difference between opportunity and obstacle
is often just our point of view.
Always keep an open mind,
even in the darkest situations.
A change in our vantage point
can reveal rich possibilities.

'What we have before us are some breathtaking opportunities
disguised as insoluble problems.'

John Gardner (1912–2002)

Now is the time to...

trust your instincts

We've spent years honing them.
Yet we rarely back them.
Look at the great painters, musicians,
singers, dancers, writers.
They have implacable faith in their instincts.
So should we.
Respect your instincts.
Nurture them.
Back them.

'Listening only to my instincts, I discovered superb things.'
Claude Monet (1840–1926)

Now is the time to...

rethink your wardrobe

Does your wardrobe do you justice?
Your clothes say a lot about you.
Shoes don't have to be expensive
but they must be clean.
Look for quality and elegance.
Choose style over fashion.
Make your own statement.

'Clothes make the man. Naked people have little or no influence on society.'

Mark Twain (1835–1910)

Now is the time to...

see a play

Leave the TV at home and head to the theatre.
Allow the stage to fire up your imagination.
Enjoy the danger of fallible actors at work.
Admire their skills.
Join their world.
Let them transport you.

'It's not the happy or tragic role that makes the difference between
actors, but the way the role is played.'

Rodney Collin (1909–1956)

Now is the time to...

show your true colours

If you believe passionately that something is right,
fight for it with all your might.
Dig deep in your soul and refuse to give ground.
Even when the odds seem overwhelming,
keep fighting.
You'll be amazed how often persistence wins the day.

'It's not the size of the dog in the fight, it's the size of the fight in the dog.'

Mark Twain (1835–1910)

Now is the time to...

follow your heart

Never underestimate the power of the heart.
When we are passionate about someone, or something,
few obstacles can defeat us.
Our hearts can inspire greatness,
sweep aside adversity,
break new ground
and draw others along with us.

'In art the hand can never execute anything higher than the heart can inspire.'

Ralph Waldo Emerson (1803–1882)

rewire

Don't retire ... rewire yourself.
Use your experience,
but keep it current.
Constantly build on your skills.
Challenge them.
Share them.
Grow.

'Experience is the best teacher, but a fool will learn from no other.'
Benjamin Franklin (1706–1790)

Now is the time to...

take a walk in the rain

Walk to its thrumming beat.
It's like nature's music.
Welcome the drops on your face.
See the way it changes things:
roads, paths, rivers, trees, flowers.
Watch as it cleanses.
Feel the sense of renewal.

'Don't threaten me with love, baby. Let's just go walking in the rain.'
Billie Holliday (1915–1959)

Now is the time to...

help the earth breathe

Find a spot crying out for new life.
Decide on the right tree for the location.
Take pleasure in planting it.
Enjoy nurturing it.
Watch it grow.
Do it again.

'The best time to plant a tree is twenty years ago. The second-best time is now.'

Anonymous

Now is the time to...

work in the garden

Like beautiful outdoor churches,
gardens encourage our spiritual natures.
They soothe our troubles and
provide stress-free havens.
They open our eyes and hearts
to growth and beauty.
They ground us.

'The best place to seek God is in a garden.'
George Bernard Shaw (1856–1950)

Now is the time to...

find your spark

We all have a spark within us
that ignites our creative spirit.
Sometimes it's overshadowed by the big obstacles
that threaten the light in our lives.
But our spark will survive our darkest times,
waiting to show the way to a brighter future.

'If the divine spark were not native to us, how could it move us to rapture?'

Johann Wolfgang von Goethe (1749–1832)

Now is the time to...

watch the clouds

Take time to watch the clouds as they decorate the sky.
See how they morph into fabulous,
ever-changing images.
Note their ephemeral beauty
and their endless patience.
Admire their stunning simplicity.
Learn their signs.
Heed their warnings.

'In the hour of adversity be not without hope, for crystal rain falls
from black clouds.'

Persian proverb

Now is the time to...

enjoy the flying flowers

How can we not be impressed by butterflies?
Despite their fragility,
and their defenselessness against the elements,
they prevail.
They exemplify the innate power of beauty.

'The butterfly is a flying flower, the flower a tethered butterfly.'
Ponce Denis Ecouchard Lebrun (1727–1807)

Now is the time to...

let in the light

Open your mind.
Open your heart.
Let light into your world.
Let it banish the darkness that sometimes engulfs us.
Let the light guide your way.

'Live happily one instant and throw not thy life to the winds.'
Omar Khayyam (1048–1131)

Now is the time to...

learn from your enemies

Too often we close our minds to our enemies.
Far wiser to view them dispassionately.
Examine their grievances.
Explore their motivations.
Balance their bias.
Distil the lessons.

`

'Have you not learned great lessons from those who braced
themselves against you, and disputed the passage with you?'
Walt Whitman (1819–1892)

Now is the time to...

let it all hang out

Sometimes you must release pent-up pressures.
Don't be half-hearted about it.
Make sure you open the valve fully.
Some do it with a primal scream.
Some let off steam with a full-on workout, run or swim.
Whatever works for you, do it.
The feeling of freedom is delicious.

'Under certain circumstances, profanity provides a relief denied even to prayer.'

Mark Twain (1835–1910)

Now is the time to...

meet your neighbours

Remember as a kid how many neighbours you knew?
How many do you know now?
Take the time to introduce yourself.
Get to know them:
learn about their lives;
meet their families;
find out what you have in common.
Help turn your neighbourhood into a community.

'There are no passengers on Spaceship Earth. We are all crew.'
Marshall McLuhan

Now is the time to...

start a journal

Make your mark. Have your say.
Start by doing it privately in your journal.
Record your thoughts and feelings:
reflect on the important things in your life.
It will grow into a valued collection
of your unique viewpoint.
When the time is right, give it to your children.
They will treasure it.

'Fill your paper with the breathings of your heart.'
William Wordsworth (1770–1850)

Now is the time to...

recapture the wonder

Chase back through the years.
Remember that sense of wonderment you had as a kid:
that driving curiosity,
that wide-eyed thirst for knowledge.
It's still there.
Sometimes it's buried under responsibilities.
Sometimes it's dulled by setbacks.
But it's still in you.
Release it.
Embrace it.

'Every child is an artist. The problem is how to remain an artist once
he grows up.'

Pablo Picasso (1881–1973)

Now is the time to...

trawl through your photos

Journey back in time,
through your treasure trove of memories.
Look deeply into the important images.
Lose yourself in them:
recall those who have made the journey with you.
Savour them.
Learn from them.

'A photo is usually looked at – seldom looked into.'
Ansel Adams (1902–1984)

Now is the time to...

turn off your phone

Cut the umbilical cord occasionally.
Take a break from the pressure of instant contact.
You can always call back later.
Set your own timetable.
Concentrate on one thing at a time.
Enjoy the freedom.

'To do two things at once is to do neither.'

Publilius Syrus (circa 46 BC)

Now is the time to...

remember a birthday

It's a lovely compliment:
a personal reaffirmation for the individual,
a rare chance for a little limelight.
For some it's a festival, for others a chilling reminder.
But all will appreciate the gesture.

'A diplomat is a man who always remembers a woman's birthday but
never remembers her age.'

Robert Frost (1874–1963)

Now is the time to...

stretch

Watch a cat or a dog.
See their languid stretches.
Notice how much they enjoy the moment.
It releases tension.
It flexes the spine.
It tones the muscles.
Exponents of yoga know the benefits.
Follow their lead.

'You're only as young as your spine is flexible.'

Bob Harper (1965–)

Now is the time to...

host a dinner party

Don't go to a restaurant.
Make the effort at home.
Even if you're not a great cook,
your guests will appreciate all your work.
The key is the company, not the food.
Learn about one another.
Enjoy the intimacy.
Watch the chemistry.

'If it were not for guests, all houses would be graves.'
Kahlil Gibran (1883–1931)

Now is the time to...

hold on to love

You'll know when it's worth fighting for:
when it's lighting your life;
when you never feel alone.
Savour it, treasure it.
And fight as hard as you can to keep it.

'The most important thing in life is to learn how to give out love, and
to let it come in.'

Morrie Schwartz (1916–1995)

Now is the time to...

try kindness

Look around you with kind eyes.
Step outside your own world.
Consider others' situations.
Chances are many are caught in desperate struggles.
You may be in a far better place.
Meet them with an open heart.

'Be kind, for everyone you meet is fighting a hard battle.'
Philo of Alexandria (20 BC–50 AD)

Now is the time to...

move on

Regrets change nothing.
They fester and infect,
but they make no positive difference.
If you can undo a wrong,
or repair a mistake,
do it.
Otherwise, learn the lesson
and look forward with renewed purpose.

'Let the dead past bury its dead!'
Henry Wadsworth Longfellow (1807–1882)

Now is the time to...

listen for the birdsong

Whether you're in the wilderness,
or in the 'Big Smoke,'
listen for the songs of birds.
Somehow, somewhere, they will be near you.
They offer a sign of optimism,
of the rhythms of nature,
of the triumph of the individual.
They sing of hope.

'How the quiet gravity of nature and her silence by contrast startles
one when one faces her collected.'
Johann Wolfgang von Goethe (1749–1832)

Now is the time to...

gaze at the winter trees

They may look sad without their leaves.
But look beyond the bare branches.
They signal nature's comforting cycles.
They represent the sure sign of regrowth.
They will blossom and bear fruit.
We all have our seasons.

'May such calm of soul be mine, so as to meet the force of
circumstances.'

Aeschylus (circa 525–456 BC)

Now is the time to...

follow through

Most of us are great starters but poor finishers.
Put yourself well ahead of the pack:
become known as the person
who always follows through.
Win a reputation for finishing all that you start.
Honour your promises.
Fulfil your commitments.

'We shall neither fail nor falter; we shall not weaken or tire. Give us
the tools and we shall finish the job.'

Winston Churchill (1874–1965)

Now is the time to...

reflect

Find some quiet time and a serene space.
Embrace the solitude.
Allow your mind to unwind
and your unconscious thoughts to roam free.
Follow them as they wander.
Surrender to the journey.

'All that is important comes in quietness and waiting.'
Rodney Collin (1909–1956)

Now is the time to...

take care

Listen to your inner warning system.
Be prudent.
Don't rush into situations
without thinking them through.
The early bird may get the worm ...
but usually it's the second mouse who gets the cheese.
Take your own advice.

'Nobody can give wiser advice than yourself.'
Marcus Tullius Cicero (106–43 BC)

listen to live music

In a prepackaged world,
the live performer stands supreme.
Whether in a great arena or a tiny pub,
the excitement of the living artist is palpable.
A great artist turns his feelings into music.
Enjoy the sensation.

'He who hears music feels his solitude peopled at once.'
Robert Browning (1812–1889)

Now is the time to...

surge

To break out of our ruts,
we usually need a quantum leap.
Otherwise we're just keeping pace,
or worse, losing ground.
Consider your situation.
Assess your position.
Calculate how big a leap you need.
Take courage.
Leap.

'Action speaks louder than words but not nearly as often.'
Mark Twain (1835–1910)

Now is the time to...

support a cause

Don't stand on the sidelines.
When a cause captures your passion,
follow your heart.
Lend your weight to it.
Fight for it.
It will widen your horizons.
It will connect your mind and heart.

'Character cannot be developed in peace and quiet.'
Helen Keller (1880–1968)

embrace the traffic

If a daily drive to work is a part of your life,
don't fight it.
Be positive.
Make it work for you.
Consider your car as a cocoon: a learning capsule.
Listen to podcasts, music, audio books,
or teach yourself a language.

'There is more to life than increasing its speed.'
Mohandas K. (Mahatma) Gandhi (1869–1948)

Now is the time to...

espresso yourself

It's not so much the coffee as the ritual.
Take a break from the raging world.
Permit yourself to relax and change pace.
Chat with friends
or savour the solitude.
Free your mind.
Smile from the inside.

'I have measured out my life with coffee spoons.'

T.S. Eliot (1888–1965)

Now is the time to...

live the present

In theory it sounds so simple.
But it's not so easy in practice.
Try living the questions in your life,
and waiting for the answers to reveal themselves.
Don't be consumed by things that may happen,
rather, enjoy the things that are actually happening.
Your time is precious.
Spend it wisely.

'How small a part of the boundless and unfathomable time is
assigned to every man? For it is very soon engulfed in the eternal.'
Marcus Aurelius (121–180)

Now is the time to...

make a budget

Think of it as a snapshot:
of your present situation and of your future.
A personal budget gives a realistic view
of your potential.
It provides a benchmark of your progress.
It shows where you can save,
and where you should trim your lifestyle
to match your income.
Take the reality check.

'Money is power, freedom, a cushion, the root of all evil, the sum of blessings.'

Carl Sandburg (1878–1967)

Now is the time to...

seek value

Don't view things by price.
They often bear no relation to genuine value.
In all things, be guided by value.
Whether objects or experiences,
consider their value to you and your real needs.
With your needs clarified, select your target,
only then compare prices.

'Price is a crazy and incalculable thing, while value is an intrinsic and indestructible thing.'

G.K. Chesterton (1874–1936)

take your own advice

Often it's easier to be wiser for others
than for ourselves.
In fact, most of us usually want corroboration
when we ask advice from others.
Most of the time we know what is right,
or the right path to follow.
When in doubt,
think how you would advise others in your position,
then take your own advice.

'It is a good divine that follows his own instructions.'
William Shakespeare (1564–1616)

Now is the time to...

change your attitude

Each day may not be a good one,
but there's something good in every day.
The difference is usually our attitude.
Look for the positive.
You'll find that the positives will shine through.
They will act as signposts to navigate
through the dark times.

'Attitude is a little thing that makes a big difference.'
Winston Churchill (1874–1965)

Now is the time to...

let yourself dream

Dreams are like micro-holidays,
whether in sleep or as daydreaming.
Some make sense of our daily lives.
Some are extensions of our hopes.
They remove our barriers.
They open possibilities.

'To come to be you must have a vision of being, a dream, a purpose, a
principle. You will become what your vision is.'

Peter Nivio Zarlenga (1941–)

Now is the time to...

break that habit

We all have our habits.
Some say they are what separate us from the herd.
But when a habit dominates,
it becomes a crutch,
an excuse to avoid living spontaneously.
It grows by unnoticed degree,
until it captivates.
Look for freedom, challenge your habit.
Drop it.
Set yourself free.

'Habit is habit, and not to be flung out of the window by any man, but coaxed downstairs a step at a time.'

Mark Twain (1835–1910)

Now is the time to...

look to the future

We don't know what the future holds.
We only know it's starting now.
Looking forward brings hope.
It can cleanse past problems and worries.
Be optimistic:
view the future through rose-coloured glasses.

'The mind is everything. What you think you become.'
Buddha (563–483 BC)

Now is the time to...

listen between the gaps

Often the key to communication is what's not said.
Listen with your ears and your eyes.
Look where the words don't match the meaning.
Don't fill the gaps by speaking;
allow the speaker to do it.
Look for motivations.
You'll be surprised at the results.

'We have two ears and one mouth so that we can listen twice as much as we speak.'

Epictetus (circa 55–135)

be curious

Knowledge won't find us, we must find it.
Every day is a chance to learn something new.
Cast your net wide,
open your mind to the excitement of learning.
Curiosity keeps us young at heart and mind.
When we stop learning, we stop living.

'I have no special talents. I am only passionately curious.'
Albert Einstein (1879–1955)

Now is the time to...

find balance

Life rushes between the mundane and madness.
Contentment is often found in moderation.
Balance is elusive.
But simply seeking it allows you to avoid excesses.
Don't make it a contest:
allow things to happen naturally.
You'll be surprised how often they centre themselves
and open up vast possibilities.

'Be moderate in order to taste the joys of life in abundance.'
Epicurus (341–270 BC)

Now is the time to...

believe in yourself

If you don't, don't expect others to.
Live up to your expectations,
not down to your doubts.
When you know you're capable,
give yourself a chance to succeed
by losing the fear of failure.
Your horizons are often self-determined.
Make sure they are as broad as your dreams.

'Whether you think you can or think you can't – you are right.'
Henry Ford (1863–1947)

Now is the time to...

rely on your common sense

It's our greatest asset in charting a course through life,
provided we listen to it.
It's the distillation of our experience.
It's our front-line defence,
our sounding board.
If something doesn't make sense,
there's usually a very good reason.

'It's a thousand times better to have common sense without
education than to have education without common sense.'
Robert G. Ingersoll (1833–1899)

Now is the time to...

set your goals

Set short-, medium- and long-term goals.
The long-term goals will keep you going
when you miss some of the short-term ones.
Goals serve as subliminal signposts.
Aiming for them takes the focus off the obstacles.
Achieving them gives you renewed enthusiasm.

'To become a champion, fight one more round.'
James ('Gentleman Jim') J. Corbett (1866–1933)

Now is the time to...

be the best you can

If you limit your vision,
you limit your possibilities.
Aim beyond your wildest dreams.
Set some seemingly impossible targets.
Then ignore all the negatives.
And turn those dreams into reality.

'Our duty, as men and women, is to proceed as if limits to or ability did
not exist. We are collaborators in creation.'
Pierre Teilhard de Chardin (1881–1955)

Now is the time to...

embrace criticism

Turn criticism into a positive.
Seek it out.
Turn it to your advantage:
ask how you, or your work, can be improved.
View the criticisms dispassionately:
use the good ones,
ignore the poor ones.

'The trouble with most of us is that we would rather be ruined by praise than saved by criticism.'

Norman Vincent Peale (1898–1993)

Now is the time to...

give back

Consider the good things in your life:
family, friends, loved ones, achievements.
We have so much for which we should be grateful.
Whenever you can, return the favour:
give something back.
Support your community, or school,
or those who helped along the way.
They'll be validated and encouraged.
You'll be gratified.

'We make a living by what we get, but we make a life by what we give.'
Winston Churchill (1874–1965)

Now is the time to...

look outside your box

Most of us live inside our daily worlds,
influenced or inspired by those within that world.
Look further afield.
Take your inspiration from unfamiliar sources.
Look through others' eyes.
You'll be surprised at the opportunities.

'A person can grow only as much as his horizon allows.'
John Powell (1963–)

Now is the time to...

be passionate about your work

Try to find work that excites your passions,
that inspires you to push your boundaries.
Strive to be the best you can at it.
Allow yourself to enjoy it.
And spread enjoyment at work.
Give it your respect.
Others will respect you in return.

'I do take my work seriously and the way to do that is to not take
yourself too seriously.'

Alan Rickman (1946–)

Now is the time to...

set your own pace

Why should you act your age?
Don't let convention set your rules.
Act the way you feel.
Stand aside from the crowd.
Follow your heart
and your instincts.

'Everyone is the age of their heart.'

Guatemalan proverb

Now is the time to...

push through adversity

If you're going through a rough patch,
spend as little time as possible there.
Consider it an opportunity to learn:
about yourself, about others, about life.
But don't linger there, or wallow in it.
Look ahead.
Keep moving.

'If you're going through hell, keep going.'
Winston Churchill (1874–1965)

Now is the time to...

value wisdom

Don't underestimate the value of knowledge,
yours or others.
Seek out those who've been there.
Ask them what they've learned.
Listen to them.
Distil their wisdom.
Apply it to your journey.

'The years teach much which the days never knew.'
Ralph Waldo Emerson (1803–1883)

Now is the time to...

search for the source

Resist the temptation to take things at face value.
Wherever possible, look beyond the obvious.
Seek out the original source.
Make your own enquiries.
Test the claims.
Make up your own mind.

'By experts in poverty I do not mean sociologists, but poor men.'
G.K. Chesterton (1874–1936)

test your limits

To find your real capabilities
you must push yourself through your comfort zone.
Don't do it recklessly.
Find what you think are your boundaries,
then challenge them by degrees.
When you see they're illusions,
push harder.

'If everything seems under control, you're not going fast enough.'
Mario Andretti (1940–)

Now is the time to...

unshackle your mind

If a problem seems insoluble:
break the rules.
Challenge your assumptions.
Change your viewpoint.
Change the questions.
Construct absurd scenarios.
Let your mind roam free.

'What the mind can conceive, the mind can achieve.'
W. Clement Stone (1902–2002)

Now is the time to...

spread hugs around

Hugs cross the language barrier.
They transmit love and warmth.
They lift hearts and spirits.
They can heal wounded souls.
They can even save a life.
Give them indiscriminately and often.

'I love hugging. I wish I was an octopus, so I could hug ten people at a time.'

Drew Barrymore (1975–)

Now is the time to...

ask 'Why not?'

When you reach an impasse on a problem,
take a new approach.
Free your mind from negativity.
Explore all possibilities, however unlikely.
Ask 'Why not?'
And follow it to its conclusion.

'Why not go out on a limb? Isn't that where the fruit is?'
Frank Scully (1892–1964)

Now is the time to...

seek self-control

Our real power comes from within.
To develop that power to full capacity,
we must have calm command of ourselves.
Learn what threatens your self-control.
Address it and conquer it.

'If passion drives you, let reason hold the reins.'
Benjamin Franklin (1706–1790)

Now is the time to...

write a personal note

Don't type it,
write it in your own hand.
It shows you really care.
It's an authentic gift in this digital world,
a personal keepsake of kindness.
It will leave a lasting impression.

'A letter is a joy of earth – it is denied to the Gods.'
Emily Dickinson (1830–1886)

Now is the time to...

row your own boat

Focus on your own efforts.
Don't be distracted by competition with others.
Aim for your personal goals.
Look inward for your motivation:
to reach your full potential,
to be your most creative.

'A creative man is motivated by the desire to achieve, not by the desire to beat others.'

Ayn Rand (1905–1982)

Now is the time to...

write your kids a love letter

When we tell our children that we love them,
it gives an invaluable boost to their self-esteem.
But writing a heartfelt letter to each of them
takes this affirmation to a new level.
Tell them how much pleasure you've received:
bringing them into the world,
watching them grow,
being part of their lives,
Give them an unforgettable memento.

'Letters are among the most significant memorials a person can leave
behind them.'

Johann Wolfgang von Goethe (1749–1832)

Now is the time to...

write your parents
a thank-you letter

Think about the sacrifices they endured for you.
Consider the countless small acts of love they gave you.
Through all the frustrations and frictions,
an unbreakable bond links you.
Don't leave it too late to thank them.
Do it in your own hand.
And straight from your heart.

'When I was a boy of 14, my father was so ignorant I could hardly
stand to have the old man around. But when I got to be 21, I was
astonished at how much the old man had learned in seven years."
Mark Twain (1835–1910)

Now is the time to...

remember what you wanted to be

Never sell yourself short.
Whatever the circumstances,
however low you feel,
recall your hopes and plans.
Use them as your benchmark:
reassess your position and aim high again.

'No bird soars too high, if he soars with his own wings.'
William Blake (1757–1827)

Now is the time to...

enjoy the journey

The crucial thing in life is the journey,
not the destination.
Focus on the trip, not the map.
Learn from the setbacks and diversions.
Use them to make yourself stronger and wiser.
Live life moment to moment.
Allow yourself to enjoy the experience.

'Experience is what you get when you didn't get what you wanted.'
Randy Pausch (1960–2008)

Now is the time to...

find your own song

Write your own lyrics.
Find your own melody.
Create your own soundtrack.
Make your own movie.
Live your own life.

'When music suitable to any scene, action, even, or environment is
played, it seems to disclose to us its most secret meaning.'
Arthur Schopenhauer (1788–1860)

Now is the time to...

develop your own traditions

Why not blaze your own trail.
Embrace the things that bring meaning to your life.
Find the things that give joy to you and your family.
Keep them as your personal traditions.
Allow others to share in your enjoyment.
Pass on your traditions.

'All change is not growth, as all movement is not forward.'
Ellen Glasgow (1873–1945)

Now is the time to...

accentuate your uniqueness

Don't dwell on the negatives in your life.
Don't allow yourself to be swamped by the crowd.
Look for the things that set you apart.
Embrace them, foster them.
Give yourself credit for them.
Hone them, improve them.
Use them to your advantage.

'Whatever you are, be a good one.'

Abraham Lincoln (1809–1865)

Now is the time to...

use the stairs

Take every chance to be active.
Avoid the elevator and the escalator.
Make the effort to use the stairs.
Feel the energy pumping through your legs, your lungs.
Use your body as it should be used.
Enjoy the glow it brings.

'A dead thing can go with the stream, but only a living thing can go against it.'

G.K. Chesterton (1874–1936)

Now is the time to...

become a storyteller

Society has a special place for the storyteller.
Take the time to develop your skills.
Listen for the stories – they're all around you.
Find their humour, their humanity and their lessons.
Take them into your heart.
Deliver them from your heart.

'What is uttered from the heart alone will win the hearts of others to your own.'

Johann Wolfgang von Goethe (1749–1832)

Now is the time to...

embrace the twilight

It is a glorious time of the day.
When the colours soften and meld into one another.
Look at the beauty of the light on a loved one's face.
Thrill to the warmth it brings to nature.
Marvel at the way it highlights skylines and buildings.
Allow the beauty to transport you.

'Colours seen by candlelight will not look the same by day.'
Elizabeth Barrett Browning (1806–1861)

Now is the time to...

find your natural sleep cycle

Experiment until you find your own sleep cycle.
Start by going to bed when you're tired.
Read until you're sleepy.
Surrender to sleep.
Wake with the sun – not to an alarm.
Start the day gently.
Take a siesta if you feel like it.
Repeat the cycle.
Feel the benefits.

'The worst thing in the world is to try to sleep and not to.'
F. Scott Fitzgerald (1896–1940)

surround yourself
with positive images

Too often we submerge ourselves in negatives.
Often it happens subliminally.
Examine your home or your workspace.
Remove the negative images.
Replace them with positives:
flowers, photos, music, scents.
Notice the change to your attitude.

'Attitude is a little thing that makes a big difference.'
Winston Churchill (1874–1965)

Now is the time to...

visit a loved one's grave

It's a great chance to reassess:
to recentre yourself.
Reflect on their life and their role in yours.
Consider how you have lived in their absence.
Honour them by reaffirming your life goals.

'To live in hearts we leave behind
Is not to die.'

Thomas Campbell (1777–1844)

Now is the time to...

write a personal mission statement

Take the time to consider your life plan.
List your goals.
Work through your priorities.
Divide them into short-, medium- and long-term.
Use them to create a mission statement:
a pithy, focused summary.
It will allow you to focus your energy
and create a road map.
Keep it flexible, visit it periodically.

'We should all be concerned about the future because we will have to spend the rest of our lives there.'

Charles F. Kettering (1876–1958)

Now is the time to...

rethink your possessions

Don't let your possessions overwhelm or control you.
After all, you're really their custodian, not their owner.
Look at them differently.
You can't take any of them with you.
So only keep things that are useful or beautiful.
Live simply.

'Simplicity is the ultimate sophistication.'
Leonardo da Vinci (1452–1519)

make a gift

The next time you want to give a gift,
don't buy it, make it.
Combine your skill with the needs of the recipient.
That will make it personal for both giver and receiver.
Let it represent your time and your talent.
Give it with love and it will be unforgettable.
Make the card yourself, too.

'The only gift is a portion of yourself.'
Ralph Waldo Emerson (1803–1882)

Now is the time to...

project ahead

When you're feeling overwhelmed by problems,
imagine you can time travel.
Project yourself ahead one year:
envision yourself in the future,
away from your current trials.
You'll be surprised how the problems
will recede in importance.

'To come to be you must have a vision of being, a dream, a purpose, a
principle. You will become what your vision is.'

Peter Nivio Zarlenga (1941–)

Now is the time to...

guard your downtime

Treasure your personal time.
It may be solitude or time with friends or loved ones.
It may be your hobby, your art or your pastime.
It's like visiting with your spirit.
Allow it to reinvigorate you.

'Cautious silence is the sacred sanctuary of worldly wisdom.'
Balthasar Gracian (1601–1658)

Now is the time to...

become an organ donor

Some see it as giving part of themselves
so another can live.
Others see it as another allowing you to live on.
Whatever way you see it,
it's your chance to make a difference to another human.
There is no greater gift.
Make sure you tell your loved ones of your decision.
Ask them to honour it.

'You give but little when you give of your possessions. It is when you give of yourself that you truly give.'

Kahlil Gibran (1883–1931)

Now is the time to...

go organic

Fight back against the chemicals
that are destroying our earth.
Cut back on processed food.
Choose organic food:
connect with the planet and the sun's energy.
It's your chance to help revitalise the earth,
and benefit the generations following us.

'When we heal the earth, we heal ourselves.'

David Orr (1944–)

Now is the time to...

re-record your answering machine

It's a small gesture.
But a strangely refreshing one.
Delete that tired, outdated message
on your voicemail or answering machine.
Replace it with a new, upbeat version.
Present a positive image.
Enjoy the satisfaction.

'Finish every day and be done with it. You have done what you could.'
Ralph Waldo Emerson (1803–1882)

Now is the time to...

look up

Take the opportunity to raise your sights – literally.
Look up from your normal field of vision:
take in the roof lines of buildings, the hills,
skies, treetops, birds.
There's a whole new world there.
It's all about changing your perspective.

'The bluebird carries the world on its back.'
Henry David Thoreau (1817–1862)

Now is the time to...

paint a mental picture

When you have the time,
close your eyes and paint with your mind.
Imagine your lover's smile.
Picture your kids at play.
Feel your mother's embrace.
Set your senses free.

'Our senses don't deceive us: our judgement does.'
Johann Wolfgang von Goethe (1749–1832)

Now is the time to...

keep your promises

Treat your word as sacrosanct.
Only promise when you believe you can deliver.
Underpromise and overdeliver.
And make good on your promise as soon as you can.
You'll be held in the highest regard.

'It's not the oath that makes us believe the man, but the man the oath.'
Aeschylus (525–456 BC)

Now is the time to...

find a mentor

A good mentor is like a compass.
It guides with compulsion.
Seek someone who can inspire your respect.
Someone with a good heart, who has wisdom
and can impart it.
But, above all, someone who continues to learn.

'What the teacher is, is more important than what he teaches.'
Karl Menninger (1893–1990)

Now is the time to...

discover people's back stories

Learn to discover people's backgrounds.
Ask and listen for the clues.
Their histories reveal many things.
They can explain fears and prejudices.
They can unravel mysteries.
They can give you warnings.
Or insights.

'The total history of almost anyone would shock almost everyone.'
Mignon McLaughlin (1913–1983)